PRINCEWILL LAGANG

Disrupt or Be Disrupted: The Entrepreneur's Dilemma

First published by PRINCEWILL LAGANG 2023

Copyright © 2023 by Princewill Lagang

All rights reserved. No part of this publication may be reproduced, stored or transmitted in any form or by any means, electronic, mechanical, photocopying, recording, scanning, or otherwise without written permission from the publisher. It is illegal to copy this book, post it to a website, or distribute it by any other means without permission.

Princewill Lagang asserts the moral right to be identified as the author of this work.

First edition

This book was professionally typeset on Reedsy.
Find out more at reedsy.com

Contents

1. Disrupt or Be Disrupted: The Entrepreneur's Dilemma   1
2. The Anatomy of Disruption   4
3. The Innovator's Mindset   7
4. From Idea to Execution   10
5. The Art of Disruptive Leadership   13
6. Navigating the Challenges of Disruption   16
7. Sustaining Disruption for Long-Term Success   19
8. The Future of Disruption   22
9. Disruption and Society   25
10. The Ethical Compass of Disruption   28
11. Nurturing Disruptive Mindsets in the Next Generation   31
12. The Continuous Journey of Disruption   34

1

Disrupt or Be Disrupted: The Entrepreneur's Dilemma

In the fast-paced and ever-evolving world of business, entrepreneurs face a dilemma that is as old as commerce itself: adapt and thrive, or resist change and risk obsolescence. This chapter explores the critical question that haunts every entrepreneur: should you disrupt the status quo, or wait to be disrupted by others? The choices you make in this regard will determine your success or failure in the dynamic landscape of entrepreneurship.

1.1 The Winds of Change

The entrepreneurial journey is a high-stakes game, where the winds of change constantly blow. In a world where technological advancements, economic shifts, and societal trends are altering the business landscape at a breakneck pace, standing still is no longer an option. As the saying goes, "Adapt or die."

1.2 The Rise of Disruptive Innovation

One of the most influential concepts in contemporary entrepreneurship is the theory of disruptive innovation, coined by Harvard Business School professor Clayton Christensen. Disruptive innovation occurs when a new entrant with a simpler, more affordable, or otherwise inferior product or service manages to upend established market leaders. Examples abound, from the transformation of the taxi industry by Uber to the overhaul of the music business by streaming services like Spotify.

1.3 The Innovator's Dilemma

Christensen's theory presents entrepreneurs with a dilemma of its own, often referred to as the "Innovator's Dilemma." Do you focus on protecting your current business model, serving existing customers, and maintaining profitability, or do you take the risky path of creating innovative, often disruptive, solutions that might cannibalize your own business?

1.4 The Risk of Complacency

Complacency is the enemy of innovation. Entrepreneurs who choose to remain complacent in the face of change risk becoming the next Blockbuster, Kodak, or Nokia—once giants in their respective industries, now cautionary tales of missed opportunities. In this chapter, we'll explore the stories of those who ignored the signs of disruption and paid the price.

1.5 The Path to Entrepreneurial Success

This chapter will also introduce you to the stories of successful entrepreneurs who embraced disruption, demonstrating that the road to entrepreneurial success often leads through uncharted territory. We'll delve into the strategies and mindsets that allowed them to not only survive but thrive in the face of disruptive forces.

1.6 The Art of Anticipation

The key to navigating the entrepreneur's dilemma is anticipation. By recognizing the signs of change, understanding market dynamics, and adopting a forward-thinking mindset, you can position yourself to be the disruptor rather than the disrupted.

1.7 A Journey of Self-Discovery

In the chapters that follow, we'll explore case studies, real-world examples, and practical advice to help you make informed decisions in the ever-evolving world of entrepreneurship. But the journey of disruption or being disrupted is not just about business—it's also a journey of self-discovery. What kind of entrepreneur are you? How do you approach risk, change, and innovation? What is your appetite for disruption?

As we embark on this exploration of the entrepreneur's dilemma, keep these questions in mind. The choices you make will not only shape your business but also define your legacy in the entrepreneurial world. The time to decide whether to disrupt or be disrupted is now.

2

The Anatomy of Disruption

In Chapter 1, we introduced the entrepreneur's dilemma and the critical decision of whether to disrupt the status quo or risk being disrupted by others. Now, in Chapter 2, we dive deeper into the intricacies of disruption, examining its various components and how it reshapes industries, markets, and entrepreneurial strategies.

2.1 Defining Disruption

Before we can fully understand disruption, we must define it. Disruption is not just a buzzword but a multifaceted concept that encompasses various dimensions. In this section, we explore the different forms of disruption, from technological and business model disruption to market and product disruption.

2.2 The Innovator's Advantage

Disruptors often have a distinct advantage: the ability to see beyond the horizon and anticipate changes in the market. We discuss how the innovator's advantage can be cultivated and used to spot opportunities for disruption before they become mainstream.

2.3 The Role of Technology

Technology is a potent force behind many disruptive innovations. We examine the pivotal role of technology in enabling change and how staying current with technological trends is crucial for entrepreneurs looking to disrupt or defend their positions.

2.4 Market Dynamics and Competition

To disrupt effectively, one must understand the dynamics of their industry and market. This section explores how market conditions, competitive landscapes, and customer behaviors influence the potential for disruption.

2.5 The Disruptor's Toolkit

What tools and strategies do disruptors use to redefine industries? We delve into the disruptor's toolkit, which includes concepts like "blue ocean strategy," open innovation, lean startup methodology, and more. These strategies and tools can empower entrepreneurs to create the change they desire.

2.6 The Domino Effect

Disruption rarely occurs in isolation. One disruptive innovation often triggers a chain reaction of changes throughout an industry or even the broader economy. We illustrate the domino effect and its implications for entrepreneurs who aim to initiate or navigate disruption.

2.7 Measuring Disruption

How can we quantify disruption and its impact on businesses and industries? We explore key performance indicators (KPIs) and metrics that entrepreneurs can use to assess the level of disruption they face or generate.

2.8 The Disruption Paradox

Disruption is not a guaranteed path to success. In some cases, attempts at disruption can lead to failure, resource depletion, or backlash from existing market players. We analyze the disruption paradox, highlighting the risks and challenges entrepreneurs face when choosing the disruptive route.

2.9 The Human Element

Behind every disruptive innovation is a team of individuals who dared to challenge the status quo. We examine the role of human capital, leadership, and organizational culture in driving successful disruption.

2.10 Case Studies

Throughout this chapter, we feature real-world case studies of companies and entrepreneurs who either successfully disrupted their industries or were themselves disrupted. These stories provide valuable insights into the strategies, decisions, and mindsets that shaped their outcomes.

As we explore the anatomy of disruption in this chapter, you'll gain a deeper understanding of what it takes to be a disruptor and how to prepare for the inevitable disruptive forces that may affect your business. Whether you're an aspiring entrepreneur or a seasoned business leader, the knowledge and insights presented here will be instrumental in making informed decisions in the ever-changing landscape of entrepreneurship.

3

The Innovator's Mindset

In Chapter 2, we delved into the intricacies of disruption and the various components that shape this transformative force in the entrepreneurial landscape. Now, in Chapter 3, we turn our attention to the heart of disruption: the mindset of the innovator. To effectively navigate the entrepreneur's dilemma, it's essential to cultivate an innovator's mindset, which will serve as your compass on the path to disruption.

3.1 The Power of Creative Thinking

Creative thinking is at the core of innovation and disruption. In this section, we explore the importance of thinking outside the box, breaking away from conventional thought patterns, and embracing creativity as a driving force in entrepreneurial success.

3.2 Embracing Risk and Uncertainty

Disruption often involves taking calculated risks and stepping into the unknown. We discuss the psychology of risk, how to manage it effectively, and the critical role of risk in the innovation process.

3.3 Continuous Learning and Adaptation

Successful disruptors are lifelong learners who thrive on adaptability. We explore the value of continuous learning, the growth mindset, and how to adapt to changing circumstances and new information.

3.4 Problem-Solving and Resilience

Every entrepreneur faces obstacles and setbacks on the path to disruption. We delve into the art of problem-solving and the importance of resilience when confronted with adversity.

3.5 Customer-Centric Innovation

Understanding and empathizing with your customers is a cornerstone of successful innovation. We examine the significance of customer-centric approaches, including design thinking, in the innovation process.

3.6 Collaborative and Open Innovation

Innovation is often a collaborative effort. We discuss the benefits of open innovation, strategic partnerships, and how working with others can amplify your innovative potential.

3.7 Ethical Considerations

Disruptors must also consider the ethical implications of their innovations. We explore the importance of ethical decision-making and corporate social responsibility in the pursuit of disruption.

3.8 Overcoming Resistance to Change

Change is met with resistance, both within and outside your organization.

We discuss strategies for overcoming resistance and garnering support for disruptive ideas.

3.9 The Art of Timing

Timing plays a critical role in successful disruption. We examine how to gauge the right moment for introducing innovative solutions and navigating industry changes.

3.10 Case Studies and Inspirational Stories

Throughout this chapter, we feature case studies and inspirational stories of innovators and entrepreneurs who have embodied the innovator's mindset. These individuals overcame challenges, embraced risk, and harnessed their creative thinking to drive change in their industries.

By the end of this chapter, you will have a profound understanding of the mindset and attributes that distinguish successful disruptors. You will also gain valuable insights into how to cultivate the innovator's mindset within yourself and your organization, equipping you to navigate the entrepreneur's dilemma with confidence and determination.

4

From Idea to Execution

In the previous chapters, we explored the entrepreneur's dilemma, the anatomy of disruption, and the innovator's mindset. Now, in Chapter 4, we shift our focus to the practical aspects of bringing disruptive ideas to life. From inception to execution, this chapter serves as a roadmap for transforming your innovative vision into reality.

4.1 Generating Disruptive Ideas

Disruption often begins with a spark of creative inspiration. We delve into techniques for idea generation, including brainstorming, problem identification, and leveraging market insights.

4.2 Market Research and Validation

Before diving headfirst into execution, it's crucial to validate your disruptive idea. We discuss the importance of market research, customer feedback, and prototype testing to ensure your concept has potential.

4.3 Business Models and Strategy

Your disruptive idea must be paired with a solid business model and strategic plan. We explore various business model frameworks, including the lean canvas and the Business Model Canvas, and discuss the strategy behind bringing your innovation to market.

4.4 Funding and Resource Allocation

Disruption requires resources, and securing funding is often a key challenge. We examine the different sources of funding, including venture capital, angel investors, and bootstrapping, and discuss strategies for effective resource allocation.

4.5 Building the Right Team

An effective team is the backbone of successful execution. We explore the importance of assembling a diverse, skilled, and motivated team and how to foster a culture that encourages innovation and embraces risk.

4.6 Prototyping and Minimum Viable Product (MVP)

Turning your idea into a tangible product or service is a critical step. We delve into the concepts of prototyping and creating an MVP, which allow you to test your innovation with minimal resources before a full-scale launch.

4.7 Scaling and Growth

Once your innovation gains traction, it's time to scale. We discuss strategies for managing growth, entering new markets, and expanding your customer base.

4.8 Risk Management and Contingency Planning

Disruption is not without risks. We examine the importance of risk management and how to develop contingency plans to address potential challenges along the way.

4.9 Intellectual Property and Legal Considerations

Protecting your innovation through intellectual property rights is essential. We explore patents, trademarks, copyrights, and other legal considerations to safeguard your disruptive ideas.

4.10 Measuring Success and Learning from Failure

Throughout the execution process, measuring success is crucial. We discuss key performance indicators (KPIs) and how to use data to make informed decisions. We also emphasize the importance of learning from failures and setbacks.

4.11 Case Studies and Real-World Examples

This chapter features a variety of case studies and real-world examples that highlight the journey from idea to execution. These stories showcase the practical application of the strategies and principles discussed.

By the end of this chapter, you will be well-equipped to take your disruptive ideas and transform them into reality. You will have a roadmap for every step of the journey, from ideation to execution, ensuring that your innovative vision can make a lasting impact on your industry.

5

The Art of Disruptive Leadership

In the previous chapters, we explored the entrepreneur's dilemma, the anatomy of disruption, the innovator's mindset, and the practical steps to bring disruptive ideas to life. Now, in Chapter 5, we shift our focus to the role of leadership in navigating the turbulent waters of disruption. Effective leadership is a linchpin for success in the face of change and innovation.

5.1 The Leadership Challenge

Disruptive leadership demands a unique set of skills and qualities. We introduce the concept of the leadership challenge in the context of disruption and explore the pivotal role that leaders play in shaping the direction of their organizations.

5.2 Visionary Leadership

Visionary leaders are those who can see beyond the immediate horizon and envision a future where their disruptive ideas have reshaped the landscape. We delve into the traits and strategies of visionary leadership.

5.3 Leading Through Uncertainty

Disruption often brings uncertainty, and leaders must navigate this with confidence and resilience. We discuss strategies for leading through uncertainty, including agile leadership and scenario planning.

5.4 Leading Innovation Teams

Effective leaders build and lead innovative teams. We explore the principles of team leadership, team dynamics, and how to foster a culture of innovation within your organization.

5.5 Change Management

Change is an inherent part of disruption, and leaders must excel in change management. We discuss change models, resistance to change, and strategies for leading your team through transitions.

5.6 Communication and Storytelling

Communication is key to rallying support and inspiring your team. We delve into the art of effective communication and storytelling, which can galvanize your organization behind your disruptive vision.

5.7 Empowering and Mentoring

Successful leaders empower their team members and provide mentorship. We examine the importance of mentorship programs and strategies for nurturing the talent within your organization.

5.8 Ethical Leadership

Ethical leadership is vital in the disruptive landscape. We explore the ethical considerations that leaders must address and the impact of their decisions on the broader community.

5.9 Leading with Resilience

Resilience is a defining trait of effective leaders in the face of adversity. We discuss resilience strategies and how to bounce back from setbacks.

5.10 Measuring and Celebrating Success

Leaders must not only drive change but also measure and celebrate success. We discuss key performance indicators (KPIs) for disruptive initiatives and the importance of recognizing achievements.

5.11 Case Studies and Leadership Examples

This chapter features case studies and examples of disruptive leaders who successfully navigated the challenges of innovation. These stories showcase the application of leadership principles in real-world scenarios.

By the end of this chapter, you will understand the critical role of leadership in the disruptive process and be equipped with the tools and insights needed to be a visionary, resilient, and ethical leader in your entrepreneurial endeavors. Effective leadership can make the difference between thriving in the face of disruption and succumbing to its challenges.

6

Navigating the Challenges of Disruption

In the preceding chapters, we explored the various facets of entrepreneurship, from the entrepreneur's dilemma to the art of disruptive leadership. In Chapter 6, we address the numerous challenges and obstacles that entrepreneurs and business leaders are likely to face when navigating the turbulent waters of disruption.

6.1 The Perils of Stagnation

Stagnation can be a silent killer of businesses, leading to irrelevance and eventual decline. We discuss the dangers of becoming complacent and the signs to watch out for in your organization.

6.2 Resistance to Change

Change is met with resistance, both within and outside your organization. We explore the sources of resistance and strategies for overcoming it.

6.3 Competition and Market Forces

Competitive pressures and market dynamics can pose formidable challenges. We discuss strategies for staying ahead of the competition and adapting to shifting market conditions.

6.4 Resource Constraints

Resource limitations, such as budgetary constraints and talent shortages, can hinder your disruptive initiatives. We examine tactics for doing more with less and leveraging available resources effectively.

6.5 Regulatory and Legal Hurdles

Regulatory and legal challenges can present significant roadblocks. We delve into strategies for navigating regulatory environments and addressing legal issues while pursuing innovation.

6.6 Technological Risks

Embracing new technologies is integral to disruption, but it also comes with risks. We discuss strategies for managing technological risks and ensuring a secure technological foundation.

6.7 Cultural and Organizational Barriers

Organizational culture and structure can either facilitate or hinder innovation. We explore strategies for fostering a culture of innovation and overcoming organizational barriers.

6.8 Failure and Setbacks

Failure is an inevitable part of the entrepreneurial journey. We discuss the importance of learning from failure, adapting, and persevering in the face of setbacks.

6.9 Sustainability and Responsibility

Disruptors must consider the environmental and social impact of their innovations. We examine the importance of sustainability and social responsibility in the disruptive process.

6.10 Coping with Success

Success can bring its own set of challenges, including managing growth and maintaining the disruptive spirit. We discuss strategies for coping with success and avoiding the pitfalls of complacency.

6.11 Case Studies and Practical Solutions

Throughout this chapter, we provide practical solutions and case studies that illustrate how entrepreneurs and leaders have effectively navigated the challenges of disruption.

By the end of this chapter, you will be well-prepared to anticipate and address the various challenges and obstacles that can arise during your entrepreneurial journey. Success in the face of disruption is not just about seizing opportunities but also about overcoming challenges with resilience and adaptability.

7

Sustaining Disruption for Long-Term Success

In previous chapters, we explored the complexities of disruption, the mindset of innovators, and the challenges entrepreneurs face when navigating the turbulent landscape of change. In Chapter 7, we delve into the strategies and approaches required to sustain disruption over the long term, ensuring that your innovations continue to thrive and make a lasting impact.

7.1 The Disruptor's Dilemma

Sustaining disruption brings its own set of challenges. We introduce the concept of the "Disruptor's Dilemma," where innovators must balance the need for ongoing innovation with the necessity of maintaining and expanding their current market share.

7.2 Continuous Innovation

Continuous innovation is the lifeblood of long-term disruption. We discuss how to foster a culture of perpetual innovation within your organization and explore strategies for idea generation and implementation.

7.3 Ecosystem Building

Successful disruptors often build ecosystems around their innovations. We examine how to create and nurture ecosystems that amplify the impact of your disruptive solutions.

7.4 Market Expansion and Diversification

To sustain disruption, you may need to expand into new markets and diversify your product or service offerings. We explore strategies for market expansion and diversification while maintaining your core disruptive focus.

7.5 Customer-Centric Evolution

Staying close to your customers and adapting to their changing needs is critical. We discuss the importance of customer-centric evolution and strategies for maintaining strong customer relationships.

7.6 Talent Attraction and Retention

A talented and motivated workforce is essential for long-term success. We delve into strategies for attracting and retaining top talent in a competitive market.

7.7 Strategic Partnerships and Alliances

Strategic partnerships and alliances can provide access to resources and expertise. We examine how to identify and cultivate partnerships that support your long-term disruption goals.

7.8 Monitoring Industry Trends

Staying current with industry trends is vital. We discuss the tools and techniques for monitoring trends and adapting to industry changes.

7.9 Ethical Considerations and Sustainability

Long-term disruptors must also consider the ethical and sustainable aspects of their innovations. We explore the importance of ethical decision-making and sustainability in the disruptive journey.

7.10 Measuring Long-Term Impact

Measuring the long-term impact of your disruption is essential for tracking progress and making informed decisions. We discuss key performance indicators (KPIs) and metrics specific to sustaining disruption.

7.11 Case Studies and Lessons from Long-Term Disruptors

This chapter features case studies and examples of organizations and leaders who have successfully sustained disruption over the long term. These stories illustrate the practical application of the strategies discussed.

By the end of this chapter, you will be well-prepared to not only initiate disruption but also to sustain it over the long term. Sustaining disruption requires a combination of continuous innovation, adaptability, and a keen understanding of the changing dynamics of your industry. With the insights and strategies presented in this chapter, you can chart a course for long-term success as a disruptor in your field.

8

The Future of Disruption

As we approach the conclusion of this book, we turn our gaze towards the future. Chapter 8 is dedicated to exploring the evolving landscape of disruption, emerging trends, and the potential opportunities and challenges that lie ahead for entrepreneurs, innovators, and business leaders.

8.1 The Acceleration of Disruption

The pace of disruption continues to accelerate. We discuss the forces driving this acceleration, including technological advancements, globalization, and changing consumer behaviors.

8.2 Emerging Technologies and Innovations

We delve into the technologies and innovations that are likely to shape the future of disruption. Topics may include artificial intelligence, blockchain, biotechnology, and other cutting-edge developments.

8.3 The Impact of Sustainability and Ethics

Sustainability and ethics are becoming increasingly prominent in the world of business. We explore how these considerations are influencing the disruptive landscape and driving new opportunities.

8.4 The Role of Regulation and Policy

Regulation and policy can either support or stifle disruption. We discuss the impact of government regulations and policies on innovation and strategies for navigating this evolving landscape.

8.5 Global Markets and International Expansion

The world is more interconnected than ever. We examine the opportunities and challenges of expanding into global markets and the role of international disruption.

8.6 The Human Element in Innovation

As technology advances, the human element remains central to innovation. We discuss the role of human creativity, empathy, and critical thinking in the future of disruption.

8.7 The Entrepreneur's Journey Ahead

The entrepreneurial journey is not static but constantly evolving. We explore what lies ahead for entrepreneurs and business leaders and how to adapt to the changing landscape.

8.8 Preparing for Disruption

We offer practical advice on how to prepare for future disruption, including how to stay informed, cultivate an innovation-centric culture, and invest in lifelong learning.

8.9 The Unpredictable Future

Despite our best efforts to predict the future, it remains inherently unpredictable. We discuss the importance of flexibility and adaptability in the face of unforeseen disruptions.

8.10 Case Studies and Visions of the Future

This chapter features case studies and visionary insights from thought leaders and organizations that are at the forefront of disruption, providing glimpses into what the future may hold.

By the end of this chapter, you will be better equipped to navigate the evolving landscape of disruption and seize the opportunities it presents. The future is filled with both challenges and possibilities, and by staying informed and maintaining an innovative mindset, you can position yourself to be a leader in shaping the future of your industry.

9

Disruption and Society

In Chapter 9, we shift our focus from the world of entrepreneurship to the broader impact of disruption on society. Disruptive innovations can have profound effects on individuals, communities, and the world at large. This chapter explores the social and ethical dimensions of disruption and the responsibilities of both entrepreneurs and society.

9.1 The Ripple Effect of Disruption

Disruption extends beyond the business world, touching various aspects of society. We examine how disruptive innovations can affect individuals, employment, communities, and entire industries.

9.2 Ethical Implications of Disruption

Disruption often raises ethical questions. We explore issues related to privacy, data security, fairness, and other ethical considerations in the context of disruptive innovations.

9.3 Inclusivity and Access

We discuss the importance of ensuring that disruptive innovations benefit all members of society. Inclusivity and access are key principles in creating a fair and equitable future.

9.4 Disruption and the Labor Force

The workforce is deeply impacted by disruptive technologies and business models. We delve into the changing nature of work, reskilling and upskilling, and the potential effects on employment.

9.5 Social and Environmental Responsibility

Sustainability and social responsibility are central to the future of disruption. We explore the role of entrepreneurs and organizations in addressing environmental and social challenges.

9.6 Regulation and Governance

Government and regulatory bodies play a role in managing disruptive innovations. We discuss the challenges and opportunities of effective regulation in the disruptive landscape.

9.7 Education and Preparing for Change

Education is a cornerstone in preparing individuals and communities for the challenges and opportunities of disruption. We explore the role of education and lifelong learning in the face of change.

9.8 The Entrepreneur's Role in Society

Entrepreneurs have a significant role to play in shaping the impact of disruption on society. We discuss the responsibilities of entrepreneurs in creating positive social change.

9.9 Case Studies and Real-World Examples

This chapter features case studies and real-world examples that highlight the social and ethical dimensions of disruption and how various entrepreneurs and organizations have addressed these challenges.

By the end of this chapter, you will have a broader understanding of the societal implications of disruption and the ethical responsibilities that come with innovative endeavors. Disruption is not just a business strategy; it's a force that can reshape the world. Entrepreneurs and innovators play a vital role in ensuring that these changes are positive, equitable, and sustainable for society at large.

10

The Ethical Compass of Disruption

In this final chapter, we delve into the ethical considerations that must guide entrepreneurs, business leaders, and innovators as they navigate the complex terrain of disruption. The ethical compass of disruption is a critical component that should underpin all actions, decisions, and strategies in the world of entrepreneurship.

10.1 The Moral Imperative of Innovation

We begin by discussing the moral imperative of innovation and how ethical considerations are central to the work of disruptors.

10.2 Ethical Frameworks for Decision-Making

Ethical frameworks provide guidance in navigating complex decisions. We explore various ethical frameworks and how they can be applied to disruption.

10.3 Transparency and Accountability

Transparency and accountability are essential in the disruptive landscape.

We discuss the importance of openness and responsibility in all actions and communications.

10.4 Privacy and Data Ethics

The collection and use of data raise significant ethical questions. We delve into the ethical considerations surrounding privacy and data ethics in the age of disruption.

10.5 Fairness and Equity

Disruption must be pursued with a commitment to fairness and equity. We examine strategies for ensuring that disruptive innovations do not perpetuate social disparities.

10.6 Social and Environmental Responsibility

Sustainability and social responsibility are paramount. We discuss the ethical obligations of entrepreneurs to address social and environmental challenges.

10.7 Ethical Leadership

Leadership plays a central role in setting the ethical tone of an organization. We explore the principles of ethical leadership and how leaders can model ethical behavior for their teams.

10.8 Ethical Challenges and Dilemmas

Ethical challenges are a part of the entrepreneurial journey. We discuss common ethical dilemmas faced by disruptors and how to navigate them.

10.9 Ethical Innovation and Impact Assessment

Assessing the ethical impact of innovation is crucial. We examine strategies for evaluating the ethical implications of disruptive initiatives.

10.10 Case Studies in Ethical Disruption

This chapter features real-world case studies of organizations and entrepreneurs who have exemplified ethical behavior and decision-making in the disruptive landscape.

By the end of this chapter, you will have a profound understanding of the ethical considerations that should guide your disruptive journey. Disruption is not just about achieving success; it's about doing so with integrity, responsibility, and a commitment to making the world a better place. Entrepreneurs and innovators have a unique opportunity to drive positive change, and this final chapter underscores the ethical imperative that should be at the core of all your entrepreneurial endeavors.

11

Nurturing Disruptive Mindsets in the Next Generation

In this penultimate chapter, we shift our focus to the future and the critical role of education and mentorship in nurturing disruptive mindsets in the next generation of entrepreneurs and innovators. Building on the insights gained throughout this book, we explore the strategies and approaches needed to inspire and guide future disruptors.

11.1 The Power of Education and Mentorship

We begin by emphasizing the transformative power of education and mentorship in shaping the entrepreneurs of tomorrow.

11.2 Fostering Creativity and Critical Thinking

Creativity and critical thinking are foundational skills for disruptive innovators. We discuss how educational institutions and mentorship programs can foster these essential abilities.

11.3 Preparing for Lifelong Learning

The pace of change demands a commitment to lifelong learning. We explore how education and mentorship can prepare individuals for continuous adaptation and growth.

11.4 Encouraging Ethical Leadership

Ethical leadership is a cornerstone of responsible disruption. We discuss how educational institutions and mentorship can instill the values of ethics and responsibility in future leaders.

11.5 Entrepreneurial Mindset Development

Developing an entrepreneurial mindset is essential. We examine strategies for promoting entrepreneurial thinking, risk-taking, and innovation in educational curricula and mentorship programs.

11.6 Diversity and Inclusion

Diversity and inclusion are critical for a thriving innovation ecosystem. We discuss the importance of fostering diverse talent and perspectives in education and mentorship.

11.7 Real-World Experience and Practical Learning

Real-world experience is invaluable. We explore the significance of internships, apprenticeships, and practical learning in the development of future disruptors.

11.8 The Role of Educational Institutions

Educational institutions play a pivotal role in nurturing disruptive mindsets.

We discuss how schools, colleges, and universities can adapt their programs to foster innovation and entrepreneurship.

11.9 The Mentor's Influence

Mentors are instrumental in guiding the next generation of disruptors. We examine the qualities and responsibilities of effective mentors.

11.10 Case Studies and Success Stories

This chapter features case studies and success stories of educational institutions, mentors, and individuals who have successfully nurtured disruptive mindsets in the next generation.

By the end of this chapter, you will appreciate the critical role of education and mentorship in shaping the future of disruption. Inspiring and guiding the next generation of disruptors is not only an opportunity but a responsibility. By fostering innovative and ethical mindsets in young individuals, we ensure a brighter future for entrepreneurship and innovation on a global scale.

12

The Continuous Journey of Disruption

As we approach the conclusion of this book, we acknowledge that disruption is not a destination but an ongoing journey. In Chapter 12, we reflect on the key takeaways, revisit the fundamental principles of entrepreneurship and innovation, and emphasize the importance of embracing change as a constant in the dynamic landscape of disruption.

12.1 The Never-Ending Story of Disruption

We begin by highlighting the ever-evolving nature of disruption and how it will continue to shape our world.

12.2 Embracing Change as a Constant

Change is the only constant in the journey of disruption. We discuss the importance of embracing change, learning from it, and using it as a catalyst for innovation.

12.3 The Call for Ethical Leadership

Ethical leadership remains a call to action. We revisit the principles of ethical leadership and the role it plays in shaping a responsible and equitable future.

12.4 The Next Disruptors

The next generation of disruptors is waiting in the wings. We reflect on the responsibility to inspire and nurture the minds that will drive the future of innovation.

12.5 A Final Word on Disruption

In this concluding section, we offer a final perspective on the incredible journey of disruption and the enduring impact it has on entrepreneurs, industries, and society as a whole.

12.6 Your Disruptive Legacy

We reflect on the legacy that each entrepreneur and innovator leaves behind, emphasizing the potential for positive change and the ethical responsibility to make a difference.

12.7 The Continuation of the Journey

This chapter closes with a message of encouragement, reinforcing the idea that the journey of disruption never truly ends, and the path forward is filled with limitless opportunities for those who dare to innovate and lead.

By the end of this final chapter, you will have a deep appreciation for the enduring nature of disruption and the ever-present potential for change and innovation. The journey of disruption is a continuous one, filled with challenges and opportunities, and it's your ethical compass, creativity, and commitment to positive impact that will guide you along the way, ensuring a brighter future for entrepreneurs, leaders, and society as a whole.

Throughout this book, we embarked on a comprehensive journey through the world of disruption and entrepreneurship. Here is a summary of the key themes and concepts explored in each chapter:

Chapter 1: Disrupt or Be Disrupted: The Entrepreneur's Dilemma
 - Introduced the critical question facing every entrepreneur: disrupt or be disrupted.
 - Explored the concept of disruptive innovation and the Innovator's Dilemma.
 - Highlighted the risks of complacency and the importance of anticipation.

Chapter 2: The Anatomy of Disruption
 - Defined various forms of disruption, including technological, market, and product disruption.
 - Explored the innovator's advantage and how technology drives disruption.
 - Discussed the disruptor's toolkit and the domino effect of disruptive innovations.

Chapter 3: The Innovator's Mindset
 - Emphasized the role of creative thinking and adaptability in fostering an innovator's mindset.
 - Discussed the importance of embracing risk, continuous learning, and resilience.
 - Explored customer-centric innovation, open innovation, and the value of collaboration.

Chapter 4: From Idea to Execution
 - Covered the steps to bring disruptive ideas to life, from ideation and market research to prototyping and scaling.
 - Discussed resource allocation, team building, and the role of leadership.
 - Highlighted the importance of risk management, intellectual property protection, and measuring success.

Chapter 5: The Art of Disruptive Leadership
  - Explored the unique leadership challenges in the disruptive landscape.
  - Discussed visionary leadership, change management, and effective communication.
  - Emphasized the role of ethical leadership, resilience, and mentoring.

Chapter 6: Navigating the Challenges of Disruption
  - Explored the challenges entrepreneurs face, including stagnation, resistance to change, and resource constraints.
  - Discussed the impact of competition, regulatory hurdles, and technological risks.
  - Emphasized the importance of sustainability and social responsibility.

Chapter 7: Sustaining Disruption for Long-Term Success
  - Examined the strategies for sustaining disruption, including continuous innovation, ecosystem building, and market expansion.
  - Discussed the role of ethical considerations, global markets, and the human element in long-term success.
  - Highlighted the importance of measuring impact and coping with the challenges of success.

Chapter 8: The Future of Disruption
  - Explored the accelerating pace of disruption, emerging technologies, and the impact of sustainability and ethics.
  - Discussed the role of regulation, the interconnectedness of global markets, and the continued significance of human creativity.
  - Examined the importance of education, adaptability, and foresight in preparing for future disruptions.

Chapter 9: Disruption and Society
  - Focused on the societal implications of disruption, including the ethical considerations, inclusivity, and access to disruptive innovations.
  - Discussed the impact on the labor force, social and environmental

responsibility, and the role of regulation.

- Emphasized the importance of education, transparency, and ethical leadership.

Chapter 10: The Ethical Compass of Disruption

- Explored the ethical imperative of innovation and ethical frameworks for decision-making.

- Discussed transparency, accountability, privacy, data ethics, fairness, and equity.

- Emphasized the role of social and environmental responsibility, ethical leadership, and impact assessment.

Chapter 11: Nurturing Disruptive Mindsets in the Next Generation

- Discussed the power of education and mentorship in shaping the future generation of disruptors.

- Focused on fostering creativity, critical thinking, inclusivity, and ethical leadership in educational institutions and mentorship programs.

- Highlighted the role of real-world experience and practical learning in developing entrepreneurial mindsets.

Chapter 12: The Continuous Journey of Disruption

- Concluded by acknowledging that disruption is an ongoing journey with ever-evolving challenges and opportunities.

- Emphasized the importance of embracing change, ethical leadership, and the responsibility to inspire and mentor the next generation of disruptors.

Throughout the book, we emphasized the ethical responsibility of entrepreneurs and innovators to drive positive and responsible change in the world of disruption. We highlighted the importance of creativity, adaptability, and ethical leadership in shaping the future of entrepreneurship. The journey of disruption is continuous, ever-changing, and filled with potential for positive impact, and it is your innovative and ethical compass that will guide you along the way.

www.ingramcontent.com/pod-product-compliance
Lightning Source LLC
LaVergne TN
LVHW010439070526
838199LV00066B/6088